Zoe McCully:
Park Ranger

Published by
Twenty-First Century Books
38 South Market Street
Frederick, Maryland 21701

Printed in the United States of America

10 9 8 7 6 5 4 3 2 1

Cover and book design by Terri Martin

Photo Credit for pages 14, 15, 17, 20, & 21:
Burt Ellsworth and Robert Miller,
The Pennsylvania Bureau of State Parks

*Dedicated to all of the working moms
who helped with this project*

Library of Congress Cataloging in Publication Data

Bryant, Jennifer
Zoe McCully: Park Ranger

Summary: Describes the life of a park ranger who is also a busy mother.
1. McCully, Zoe—Juvenile literature. 2. Park rangers—United States—
Biography—Juvenile literature. 3. Working mothers—United States—
Biography—Juvenile literature.
[1. McCully, Zoe. 2. Park rangers. 3. Working mothers.]
I. Brown, Pamela, 1950- ill. II. Title. III. Series: Working Moms.
SB481.6.M33B79   1991   333.78'3'092—dc20 [B] [92]   90-24371 CIP AC
ISBN 0-941477-54-1

Zoe McCully:
Park Ranger

Jennifer Bryant
Photographs by Pamela Brown
Photographic Consultant: Bill Adkins

TWENTY-FIRST CENTURY BOOKS
FREDERICK, MARYLAND

A warm fall breeze rustles the last colorful leaves of the year. Overhead, a flock of geese decides that this November weekend is a good time to begin flying south. And in Zoe McCully's house, six-month-old Ian is beginning to open his eyes on a new day.

For most people, fall means an end to summer vacation. It means a time to get back to school or the office. But that's not what it means for Zoe McCully. When fall comes to eastern Pennsylvania, Zoe heads to the park.

For most people, weekends mean a time to have fun. Many people like to get outdoors, perhaps to spend the day at a nearby park—hiking along the scenic trails, boating or fishing on the lakes, or picnicking in the bright sunshine.

But not Zoe McCully. She heads to the park to work.

Zoe McCully is a park ranger. It's her job to make sure that the natural beauty and resources of Marsh Creek State Park are preserved for everyone to enjoy.

But Zoe is also a mom, and this morning (like most mornings) she is awakened by the familiar sound of Ian's crying. "As regular as an alarm clock," Zoe mumbles as she wipes the sleep from her eyes and finds her half-awake way to the nursery. It's 6:30 in the morning. "I know I'll get used to this routine," she says to herself. Zoe cradles the baby in her arms and settles herself in the family's old rocking chair. "But when?" she asks, as she begins to nurse Ian.

The motion of the rocking chair lulls mother and child into a quiet, peaceful rhythm. Zoe's thoughts turn to the busy day ahead.

Today is Saturday, a day off for most people. The first rays of morning sunshine filter through the curtains of the nursery window. Zoe knows that it's going to be a nice day today. And she also knows that the state park is going to be crowded. It's not going to be a day off for her. When most people are away from school or work, that's when Zoe and the other rangers at Marsh Creek have to work the hardest.

At 7 o'clock, it's time for the baby's bath. "Good morning," says Zoe's husband, Mark, as he pokes his head into the nursery. "Need any help in here?"

 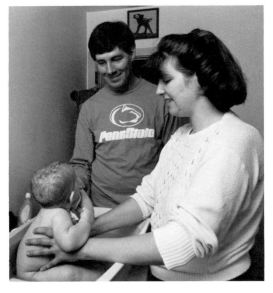

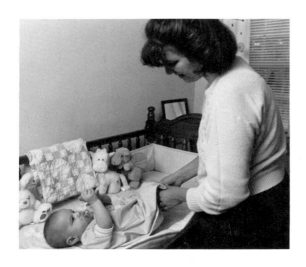

"We're just about done," replies Zoe. "Why don't you wake up Sarah while I start breakfast?"

"Can I get out of my pajamas first?" Mark laughs. "Just give me a second."

7

Upstairs, Mark changes and gets ready for the day. "I like taking care of the kids," he says. "I don't even mind changing diapers, now that I've finally figured out which end is which." In the meantime, a sleepy seven-year-old named Sarah waddles into the room. "Well, look who's up now," Mark says. "It's the big sister." Sarah comes over to her daddy for a good-morning visit.

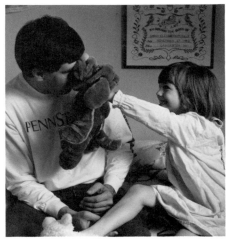

Downstairs, Zoe is busy in the kitchen. Toast, eggs, and juice are on the menu this morning. While Zoe stirs the eggs and butters the toast (and adds cinnamon for Sarah), Katrina strolls in from the living room, where she's been sleeping on the sofa.

Katrina is the family's cat, though she thinks of herself as one of the family.

"I guess you want breakfast, too," Zoe says, bending down to rub behind Katrina's ears. Katrina stretches with pleasure and softly purrs, as if to say, "Yes, that sounds good to me."

"Breakfast, everyone!" Zoe announces. The clock on the stove reads 7:30 A.M.

The sound of Mark's heavy footsteps on the stairs followed by the pitter-patter of Sarah's bunny slippers makes Zoe chuckle.

"I wish I could spend all morning at home," Zoe says to herself. "But I'm glad that Mark is here to take care of the kids while I'm at the park."

Saturday morning is a special time for the McCullys.

It's a time for old tricks.

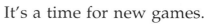
It's a time for new games.

It's a time for hanging around.

It's a time for just hanging out.

But it's not a time that lasts forever. When the morning sun has chased away the last of the shadows from the back yard, it's time for Zoe to get ready for work.

"I hate to spoil the fun," Mark says suddenly, "but it's almost 10 o'clock."

"Already?" Zoe asks.

"Already?" Sarah asks, too.

Zoe hurries to pack her lunch and iron her uniform.

At 10:30 A.M., it's time to go to work. But Zoe takes time for one last good-bye hug from Ian and Sarah.

It's a short drive to the park. In just a few minutes, Zoe pulls up to the park gate. A line of cars is already waiting to enter. "It really *is* going to be a busy day," Zoe thinks. She quickly finds a parking space near the park office. Grabbing her ranger's hat and her brown-bag lunch, she hurries inside.

Marsh Creek State Park is 1,200 acres of rolling hillside nestled in the southeastern corner of Pennsylvania. The clear water of Marsh Creek Lake adds another 500 acres to the park. It's a park that seems to have something for everyone. There are miles of trails for hiking and horseback riding. For those who prefer water sports, there's sailing, swimming, and canoeing. There's fishing and hunting during certain seasons. And for people who just like to take it easy on a long, lazy afternoon, there are plenty of picnic spots and camping areas.

But Marsh Creek is not just a park for summertime fun. When the winter months have covered the trails and picnic areas with snow, there's sledding, tobogganing, and cross-country skiing. And when the cold weather has finally frozen Marsh Creek Lake, you can skate on it, or boat on it, or even cut a hole in the ice and go winter fishing.

It certainly seems that Marsh Creek State Park has something for everyone. But Marsh Creek is much more than an outdoor playground. It provides people with more than just a place to have outdoor fun.

Perhaps you've visited a park with your family or friends. And you've probably heard of such famous parks as Yellowstone, the Grand Canyon, or the Everglades. But have you ever stopped to think about what a park really is? Have you ever wondered why we have parks?

Like many other parks, Marsh Creek isn't just for people. It's also a home for many animals. There are deer in the woods, and rabbits, squirrels, raccoons, snakes, and many other animals. Pheasants and ducks nest in the thick grasses, and many kinds of birds find safety in the tall trees. Turtles and frogs enjoy the marshy areas along the banks of the lake. For thousands of ducks, geese, and other waterfowl, Marsh Creek Lake is a stopover point on their annual migrations. And for the fish—catfish and bass, walleye and crappies, muskies and panfish—the lake is a home all year long.

There's even more to Marsh Creek. In a world where there always seem to be new highways, and new shopping centers, and new housing developments, Marsh Creek State Park is a place where our natural resources—the trees, the grasses, the water—are protected and preserved. It's a place where you can still swim in clean water, and breathe fresh air, and see the stars come out at night. It's a place where you can escape the crowded, busy cities and see nature at work.

A park is all of these things: it's a place for long days of outdoor fun, a home for countless animals, and an important natural resource. That's what a park is really about. And that's why we have parks: to preserve the natural environment for public enjoyment.

As a park ranger, Zoe has to keep in mind the park's goals. Part of her job is to make sure that people have a safe place to enjoy outdoor activities. And part of her job is to teach people to preserve the balance of the park's natural environment. "It's like being a teacher and a police officer at the same time," Zoe says. "It's not always an easy job."

It is always a busy job. Today is no different.

Inside the park office, Zoe receives her day's assignments. "I'm glad to see you," her supervisor, Larry, says. "There's a lot to do. You'll be working with Paul today. I'd like you to make a 'round' of the park. And check the dam on your way back."

Zoe gets ready to meet her partner, but Larry remembers another job that needs to be done. "And one more thing," he continues, looking a bit worried. "Pay close attention to the hiking trails on the south side. We had a report of gunshots over there last night. Better check it out."

Again, Zoe begins to leave the office, but Larry looks like he's trying to think of something else. "Oh, yes," he says at last, "I've scheduled you for a guided nature walk later this afternoon. I knew you'd enjoy that." Zoe is unsure whether that is her last assignment for the day or not. "Well, don't you think you'd better get going?" Larry says with a smile.

In a few minutes, Zoe and her partner, Paul, are driving a park patrol car along the waterfront road. From the car window, Zoe can see the sailboat-dotted lake. Strong, steady winds make Marsh Creek a good place for wind-surfing, too.

As Zoe and Paul drive along, they spot families setting
up for afternoon picnics. Other people are launching boats
from the park's dock or fishing from the grassy banks.

It's the job of a ranger to enforce the park rules. No motorboats on the lake, no dumping trash, no picking wildflowers, no fishing without a license—these are just a few of the many regulations that keep Marsh Creek a safe place for everyone and preserve its natural resources. To some of the park's visitors, these rules may seem to be a nuisance. But to the rangers, they're very important. These rules protect the life of the park.

"Gasoline-powered engines would quickly pollute the lake," Zoe explains, "and trash is a health hazard to the animals who live in the park. It's important to remember that Marsh Creek is a natural ecosystem. It's a community of living things where each animal or plant has a special place and purpose. Each living thing here is connected in many ways to the rest of the ecosystem. Marsh Creek is a good example of the natural network of living things."

"When people come to the park," Zoe continues, "they become part of the ecosystem. But too many people can upset the natural network. That's why we limit the number of cars that enter the park each day. That's why we limit the number of fishing licenses assigned each year. And that's why we make these daily patrols. It's not just to see that the park rules are enforced. It's to make sure that the park itself is protected and preserved for future visitors to enjoy."

On their way around the park, Zoe and Paul stop several times to answer questions. What size fish can we keep? Where's the best place to watch birds? Do we have to stay on the hiking trails? What kinds of deer live in the park? Can we launch our boat from the shore? "We try to do more than just answer these questions," Zoe says.

"We try to educate our visitors, to show them how living things are connected to one another. We try to explain what this park is really about."

As a young girl, Zoe McCully learned the lessons nature has to teach. She attended a summer nature camp, where she took courses in water safety and wilderness survival. When Zoe was only 13 years old, she became a counselor at the camp, and by the time she was in high school, she was made the assistant director. "It didn't seem like work to me," Zoe remembers. "I loved learning about nature and passing on my knowledge to others. Today, that's still my favorite part of the job."

"I may be a teacher and a police officer all rolled into one," she says, "but I like the teaching part best."

For a future park ranger, Zoe had a good role model. Her father, a school teacher, worked as a seasonal park ranger each summer. "By the time I was out of high school," Zoe recalls, "I knew I wanted to become a ranger, too."

In college, Zoe took courses in the Parks and Recreation program. Her studies included botany (the study of plants), dendrology (the study of trees), conservation (protecting natural resources such as forests and waterways), and animal husbandry (the care of animals). "Park rangers must have a strong commitment to the environment," Zoe says. "It's important for us to know how each part of a natural ecosystem works—and works with other living things in a careful balance. It's important for us to know how living things adapt to changes in the ecosystem. Above all, park rangers must respect the natural order of the environment."

But Zoe also took several "people-related" courses: psychology and sociology (the study of human behavior), recreation law (the rules under which parks are managed), and environmental education (teaching people about the natural world). "In college, I learned that very few park rangers work only in the wilderness, far away from people," Zoe explains. "Public parks are for people to enjoy, and most park rangers are in constant contact with the public. So they need training in human behavior and education."

"These days, with more and more people using parks for recreation, good 'people' skills are very important for us," says Zoe. "Most of the visitors here are pleasant and follow the rules. Many of them are also eager to learn about their natural surroundings. But there are always a few who abuse the privilege of using the park. They break our rules and endanger the fragile balance of this natural ecosystem."

During her final year of college, Zoe was required to do a three-month internship, or training session, at a state park. She was assigned to the Laughing Brook Wildlife Sanctuary and Education Center in Massachusetts. There she learned the many different skills that she would use as a ranger at Marsh Creek: creating a wildlife education program for the public, leading group discussions on ecology, giving water rescue and safety courses, and helping to plant 50 acres of young forest for wildlife habitats and erosion control.

She also learned how to treat and take care of wounded and abandoned wild animals: birds, rabbits, squirrels, and even a few bears. "Most of them were released back into the forest when they were healthy and strong enough," Zoe observes. "But sometimes I used the younger ones in the park's educational programs."

"The park's educational programs were especially helpful for the city youngsters who visited regularly," Zoe says with obvious pride. "I took them camping, canoeing, and hiking. I taught them how to survive in the forest— where to find shelter, what plants and berries are safe to eat, and how to build a campfire. Coming from a crowded and sometimes dangerous environment, many of these children had no idea what they were getting into."

"But out in the woods," Zoe says, "they began to feel free and safe. They also began to gain self-confidence by learning how to take care of themselves and their world. And they saw, perhaps for the first time, that there is a natural order in the world and that everything—and everyone—has an important and special place in it. I guess you could say that these kids came to see that they are part of an ecosystem, too."

"This lesson is one of the many wonderful gifts nature has to offer," Zoe adds.

It's almost 2 o'clock. Zoe and Paul drive past the fields on the east side of the park. Zoe calls the park office. "We're heading to the dam," she reports. The dam, which was built in 1973, is part of the area's water management program. By blocking up the Brandywine River and creating Marsh Creek Lake, the dam prevents flooding and water shortages.

Zoe steers the patrol car onto the steep, gravel road that leads to the dam. She stops next to a round, concrete building where the dam's controls are located. Each day, the rangers must check the water level of the lake. If the water level is too high or too low, the valves which regulate the flow of water in and out of the lake will have to be adjusted.

Back in the patrol car, Zoe and Paul head to the hunting area on the north side of the park. As they leave the lake behind, Zoe notices that the wind has increased. Dozens of wind-surfers are crisscrossing the water, and the brightly colored sails have turned the lake into a rainbow of color. Zoe watches one expert surfer skim quickly toward the bank, then suddenly turn and head back to the open water. "Someday, when I have more time, I'll learn to do that, too!" she says to herself.

Ten minutes later, Zoe and Paul are walking along the trails that lead deep into the north woods. After a few minutes of searching, they find what they are looking for: four empty bullet shells.

Paul picks them up and hands them to Zoe. She inspects them and then puts them in her pocket. "Larry will want to see these," she says.

Unlike some parks, hunting is legal at Marsh Creek. "Hunting is part of our wildlife management program," explains Zoe. "If we didn't allow hunting, the animal populations would get too large. There wouldn't be enough food for all of them, and many would starve. Hundreds of years ago, these animals were hunted by other animals like wolves and mountain lions. Now man has taken over the role of predator. Man has become part of the ecosystem."

"But hunting is only allowed during certain weeks of the year and only in certain parts of the park," Paul adds. "Whoever was shooting in this part of the park was breaking the regulations—and putting everyone in danger. We'll have to patrol this area of the park more carefully."

It's 3:30 P.M. when the patrol car rolls past the main entrance of the park once again. Zoe takes some time now to prepare for her afternoon nature walk. The nature walk is the kind of activity that Zoe finds so rewarding. When she was first hired at Marsh Creek, she designed a self-guided nature trail. She laid out a half-mile path through the woods and set up checkpoints along the way. She marked each checkpoint with a sign that identifies the kinds of plants and animals found there. Now, simply by taking a short walk, visitors can learn more about their environment.

When she first came to work at Marsh Creek, Zoe was the only female ranger. Some of the men treated her differently because she was a woman. "They kept carrying things for me and opening gates for me on the trails," Zoe recalls. "On foot-patrol, when we were out in bad weather, they'd ask me if I was too tired or cold. I don't think they meant to be disrespectful. They didn't know what to expect. Finally, I told them that I wanted to do my share of the physical work. I told them that I was happy to be working outdoors—in all kinds of weather!"

Like Zoe, many women today are choosing careers in the field of parks and recreation. And, like Marsh Creek, many state and local parks offer part-time and seasonal employment. Both women and men with families find this kind of flexibility an advantage.

When she became pregnant with Ian, Zoe stopped working at the park for several months. But she kept busy at home designing a nature workshop for public school teachers and a wildlife slide presentation for their students. "When Ian is older and I go back to work full-time," she says, "I hope to visit some schools and see these programs in action."

For now, though, Zoe accepts the fact that she can't do everything she wants to do. "I'm the kind of person who likes to do one thing at a time," she says. "If I'm doing too many things at once, then I don't feel like I'm doing any of them very well. Knowing this about myself, I made the decision to work part-time while the children are young. Looking back, I know it was the right choice for me. I'm still involved in my career, but most of my time and energy now go to my family."

When Mark and Zoe decided to have children, they both knew there would have to be changes. A family is like an ecosystem: when something is added or changed, it has an effect on everyone. But families, like ecosystems, can adapt. "It was my decision to work only part-time at the park," Zoe says. "That decision wasn't based on any one thing, but rather on a combination of different thoughts and feelings. It just seemed like the right thing to do for me and my family."

At 4 o'clock, Zoe meets her group by the giant oak tree. She introduces herself and tells the children a little bit about the park and her job. She shows them a map of the lake area and explains how the park's ecosystem stays in balance. "Every plant and animal has a place in the natural order of things at Marsh Creek," she carefully explains, "from the tiniest minnow to the largest white-tailed deer. I'd like you to follow me now as I show you some of the more common plants and animals."

The children follow eagerly. They cross an open field and then walk down a shady, wooded path. Along the way, Zoe stops to point out several signs of wildlife nearby: a fox's den, a narrow deer path through the woods, a bird's nest hidden deep in the tall grasses.

"How do the deer know which berries are good to eat?" the children want to know. "What are baby foxes called?" "Where does a rabbit live?" "What kind of bird is that?"

Zoe patiently answers each of these questions and many more. Teaching children about nature is what she likes to do best. And even though it's near the end of her work shift, Zoe feels like she's just begun. "My energy gets restored when I'm teaching," she says. "This is so much fun that I don't even think of it as work."

At the end of their walk, Zoe uses her net to catch
a few monarch butterflies. The children listen as she tells
them about the migration and eating patterns of these
remarkable insects.

"Speaking of eating, who would like some refresh-
ments?" Zoe finally asks, as she lets the butterflies go. The
children enjoy their snack, and Zoe has some more time to
teach them about Marsh Creek.

"I hope you'll come back to visit us again!" she tells the
group as they walk back to the office to meet their parents.

It's 5 o'clock: time for Zoe to say good-bye to her partner, her boss, and her park. Her work at the park is finished for the day.

Driving home, Zoe has time to think about what she has accomplished. "Being a park ranger is different from being a construction worker, a writer, or a painter. At the end of their day, they can look at their work and say to themselves, 'I did a good job on this building, this book, or this picture.'"

"But rangers just have to know that they did their best to preserve the environment for people to enjoy."

Zoe has that feeling today. As she drives past the lake, she glimpses a pair of blue herons nesting on the bank. "We must be doing a good job," Zoe thinks.

As she steers the car along the gravel drive to her home, Zoe's thoughts turn to the evening ahead. There's lots of work yet to do: "Make dinner and clean up, bathe Ian and read Sarah a story, put the kids to bed. There's always some-thing to do."

"But that's what makes being a working mom such a challenge," Zoe thinks as she steps onto the front porch. "I wouldn't have it any other way!"

Glossary

adapt	how living things respond to changes in the environment
animal husbandry	the care and raising of animals; the management of animal resources
botany	the study of plants
conservation	the protection and preservation of natural resources
dendrology	the study of trees
ecology	the study of living things in their environment
ecosystem	a community of living things and their environment
environment	the world in which a living thing makes its home
environmental education	the kind of teaching that instructs people about the natural world
erosion	how wind and water remove soil from the earth's surface
habitat	the place where a living thing makes its home
migration	the movement of animals from one place to another
park	an area set aside for public use; a park preserves the natural environment for public enjoyment
predator	an animal that kills and eats other animals
preservation	how an environment is kept in its natural condition
ranger	a park official who helps preserve natural resources
recreation law	the rules under which public parks are managed
wildlife	animals and plants living in a natural environment